for Asha and Samir
A whirl wind tour is what you get
Here's your Chicago alphabet!

# W is for Windy City

## A Chicago Alphabet

Written by Steven L. Layne and Deborah Dover Layne
Illustrated by Michael Hays and Judy MacDonald

*Michael Hays*        *Judy MacDonald*

*For Charles and Gail Dover—*
*Dad and Mom—who know a lot about Chicago…*
*and even more about leading a family.*

Love, Steve and Debbie

*For Dr. Margaret Burroughs who gave Chicago the DuSable Museum*
*and now in her nineties asks us what our legacy will be.*

—Michael Hays

*For Mom and Dad—*
*my favorite Chicago natives.*

—Judy MacDonald

Text Copyright © 2010 Steven L. Layne and Deborah Dover Layne
Illustration Copyright © 2010 Michael Hays and Judy MacDonald

**Sleeping Bear Press**
315 E. Eisenhower Parkway, Ste. 200
Ann Arbor, MI 48108
www.sleepingbearpress.com

© 2010 Sleeping Bear Press is an imprint of Gale, a part of Cengage Learning.

Printed and bound in China.

*First Edition*

10 9 8 7 6 5 4 3 2 1

Library of Congress Cataloging-in-Publication Data

Layne, Steven L.
W is for Windy City : a Chicago alphabet / written by Steven L. Layne and
Deborah Dover Layne ; illustrated by Michael Hays and Judy MacDonald.
p. cm.
ISBN 978-1-58536-420-6
1. Chicago (Ill.)—Guidebooks—Juvenile literature. 2. Alphabet books—
Juvenile literature. I. Layne, Deborah Dover. II. Hays, Michael, 1956- ill.
III. MacDonald, Judy, 1963- ill. IV. Title.
F548.33.L39 2010
917.73'110444—dc22
2009040872

90

94

Lincoln ★
Park Zoo

N Lake Shore Dr.

Magnificent Mile

★ John
Hancock
Center

★ Navy Pier

W Grand Ave

★ Harpo
Studios

★ Art Institute
of Chicago

★ Willis Tower

290

★ Harold
Washington
Library

★ Grant Park

CHICAGO

W Roosevelt Dr

S. Michigan Ave

S Lake Shore Dr

Shedd ★
Aquarium

★ Adler
Planetarium

LAKE
MICHIGAN

CHICAGO

W Cermak Rd

90

94

55

CHICAGOLAND

A is for Art Institute
or Adler Planetarium.
And if we want a "triple A"
we'll add the Shedd Aquarium.

The Adler Planetarium and Astronomy Museum in Chicago was the first planetarium built in the western hemisphere and is the oldest in existence today. Since the museum's opening in 1930, visitors view representations of the night sky in the historic Sky Theater. It is part of Chicago's Museum Campus along with the Shedd Aquarium and the Field Museum of Natural History.

When the John G. Shedd Aquarium officially opened on May 30, 1930, it housed the greatest variety of sea life under one roof in the world. More than 75 years later it has been restored and updated, and is now considered a historic landmark. The aquarium is a conservation leader around the world.

The Art Institute of Chicago is located in Chicago's Grant Park. At one million square feet, it is the second largest art museum in the United States behind the Metropolitan Museum of Art in New York. The two bronze lions that flank its entrance were made for the building's opening in 1893. Find interesting information about these museums via the Web at www.adlerplanetarium.org, www.sheddaquarium.org, and www.artic.edu.

A a

Barack Obama is the **B**
who left Chicago for D.C.
He opened up the White House door
as president number forty-four.

# Bb

Barack Obama is the 44th president of the United States. He is the first African-American to hold the office. Mr. Obama was the junior United States Senator from Illinois from January 2005 until November 2008, when he resigned following his election as president.

Mr. Obama was born on August 4, 1961, in Honolulu, Hawaii. He is a graduate of Columbia University and Harvard Law School, where he was the first African-American president of the *Harvard Law Review*. He laid down roots in Chicago after graduating from Columbia. He worked as a community organizer in Chicago prior to earning his law degree and practiced as a civil rights attorney in Chicago before serving three terms in the Illinois Senate. From April to October 1992, Mr. Obama directed Project Vote! in Illinois. It achieved its goal of registering 150,000 of 400,000 unregistered African-Americans in the state. He also taught constitutional law at the University of Chicago Law School from 1992 to 2004.

# C c

Chicago Cubs, a double C,
will surely live in infamy.
For though it's known they often lose,
they're still the team that most fans choose.

Two baseball teams call Chicago home. On the south side, the Chicago White Sox play at U.S. Cellular Field (formerly Comiskey Park). But around the world, since 1876, Chicago is known for its beloved Cubs. The Cubs have played at the "Friendly Confines of Wrigley Field" since 1914. The team won the World Series in 1908.

According to legend, the owner of a restaurant and his goat tried to attend a Cubs game in 1945. The man was denied entrance to the game by an usher who declared, "No goats allowed." The restaurant owner put a curse on the team. "You Cubs will never win another world championship," he said angrily. The Cubs have not won a world series since that time.

Baseball is not the only game in town. Sports fans can catch the Bulls playing basketball and the Blackhawks playing hockey at the United Center. For football fans, the Bears are Chicago's team. Soldier Field is home to both the Bears and the Chicago Fire, the city's major league soccer team.

Elected to his first term as mayor of Chicago in 1955, Richard J. Daley was known as one of the most powerful political leaders in the United States. As a young man he received both undergraduate and law degrees from Chicago's DePaul University. Daley was elected to the Illinois House of Representatives in 1936 and later served in the Illinois Senate and as State Revenue Director. He was reelected as mayor five times.

The premier civic center in the city of Chicago is also named after him. The Richard J. Daley Center, also known by its courtyard called Daley Plaza, houses more than 120 court and hearing rooms as well as the official law library of the City of Chicago.

Richard M. Daley, son of the famous mayor, was first elected mayor of Chicago in 1989. Like his father, he has had a long run as mayor and was most recently reelected in November of 2007.

The Daleys of Chicago are each a famous D. They're the "most-elected" mayors in the city's history.

D d

Chicago's Elevated Train, known as the "El" or "L" (which is short for the word "elevated"), circles Chicago's central business district which Chicagoans refer to as "The Loop." Streetcar tracks once looped around the downtown area, so citizens began calling that area "The Loop."

Very scenic and often noisy, these train cars have carried passengers over Wabash Avenue, Van Buren, Wells, and Lake Streets for over 100 years. The cost of a ride on the "El" has risen from five cents in the early 1900s to close to two dollars today. The Chicago Transit Authority, also known as the CTA, operates six commuter lines in downtown Chicago.

E e

The story of our **E**, the "El,"
won't fall between the cracks.
These famous trains are nicknamed
for their elevated tracks.

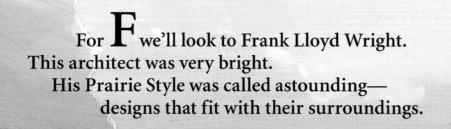

For F we'll look to Frank Lloyd Wright.
This architect was very bright.
His Prairie Style was called astounding—
designs that fit with their surroundings.

Frank Lloyd Wright was a famous architect who made his home in the suburbs of Chicago. He came to Chicago in the 1880s. Wright developed his influential Prairie Style of architecture which consisted of long, low, flat buildings designed to reflect the landscape of the Midwestern plains. He was also well known for incorporating many elements of nature into his designs. Many of Wright's works are located in the Chicago suburb of Oak Park. His best-known design in the city of Chicago itself is Robie House. This house was built in 1909 and is located near the University of Chicago. Robie House became a National Historic Landmark in 1963.

In the 1800s most of Chicago's buildings were wooden, making them perfect kindling for what is known today as the Great Chicago Fire of 1871. The fire began on DeKoven Street when, according to legend, a cow kicked over a lantern in Mrs. O'Leary's barn. Fanned by strong winds, the flames raced north and east through the city. The fire raged for more than 24 hours. It wiped out the downtown area and most north side homes. It killed at least 300 people, left more than 90,000 homeless, and destroyed millions of dollars' worth of property.

The Pillar of Fire sculpture, created by Egon Weiner in 1961, stands on DeKoven Street at the very spot where the Great Chicago Fire started. It is a visual reminder of the hope and courage Chicagoans displayed as they rebuilt this great city up from the ashes of the devastating fire.

The city's greatest tragedy,
the Great Chicago Fire is G.
It's only legend that somehow
it started with O'Leary's cow.

**H** is Harpo Studios,
which rules the talk show scene,
'cause Oprah is its owner
and she's Chicago's queen.

Millions of people in America and around the world watch the *Oprah Winfrey Show* each weekday. The award-winning talk show debuted in Chicago in 1986 and is hosted by one of the nation's most successful entertainers—Oprah Winfrey.

In 1988 Oprah bought a former armory and transformed it into a state-of-the-art production facility she named Harpo Studios. Where did the name come from? Harpo is Oprah spelled backward. The studio takes up a full city block.

Oprah is famous for her humility and generosity. She has dedicated her show to topics that will help her viewers live happier, more productive lives. Oprah's charity work is legendary. She does not just donate money, she believes in getting involved and doing the necessary work it takes to help others. Oprah's Angel Network was founded on a simple idea—that we all have the power to make a difference. Oprah was once quoted as saying, "My first day in Chicago—September 4, 1983. I set foot in this city, and just walking down the street, it was like roots, like the motherland. I knew I belonged here."

# I i

Chicago has the distinction of being the birthplace for many famous inventions including steel frame skyscrapers, elevated railways, Cracker Jack™, the zipper, and Tinkertoys™.

Charles Pajeau and Robert Pettit designed the first Tinkertoys™ in the early 1900s after watching children playing with pencils and old spools of thread. At Christmastime the men marketed their toys by having people in elf costumes play with Tinkertoys™ in a display window at a Chicago department store. A year later, over one million sets had been sold.

A unique popcorn, peanuts, and molasses confection that was the forerunner to Cracker Jack™'s caramel-coated popcorn and peanuts was introduced by F.W. Rueckheim at the World's Columbian Exposition in 1893, Chicago's first World's Fair.

In 1893 Whitcomb Judson of Chicago marketed a "Clasp Locker" (an early version of the zipper), a complicated hook-and-eye shoe fastener. Judson thought this invention would save people time by fastening their shoes with one hand. Years later the B.F. Goodrich Company coined the name "zipper" in 1923 and it slowly became more popular for use in clothing.

I is for Inventions
loved by girls and boys.
Chicago's birthed some famous ones;
among them—Tinkertoys™.

Michael Jeffrey Jordan grew up in Wilmington, North Carolina. He loved sports from the time he was a little boy. Michael decided to play basketball when he was in high school but did not make the varsity team at first. Michael Jordan did not give up. He practiced and worked hard. He made the team the next year.

During his freshman year at the University of North Carolina, Michael made the winning basket in the championship game of the 1982 NCAA basketball tournament. He entered the professional ranks playing with the Chicago Bulls and was named NBA Rookie of the Year.

Michael's amazing ability to fly and soar on the basketball court earned him the nickname "Air Jordan." He led the NBA in scoring average a record 10 seasons, including 8 consecutive seasons. The NBA's Most Valuable Player award was bestowed upon him 5 times. Michael's average of 30.12 points per game is the highest in NBA history. He also led the United States to two Olympic gold medals. The hallmark of this great Chicago athlete's success was his "never give up" attitude.

J j

Throughout the 1990s
the **J** that reigned on high
was Chi-town's Michael Jordan
exploding from the sky.

# K k

McDonald's™ serves up quite a **K**.
Its founder, Mr. Kroc, is Ray.
He gave fast food a famous brand
headquartered in Chicagoland.

McDonald's™ was founded in 1955 by Ray Kroc. At the time, Mr. Kroc was a distributor of machines that made milk shakes. He learned about a hamburger stand in California that had eight of these machines. It was called McDonald's™. Ray visited the stand and was impressed by how quickly people were served. Mr. Kroc persuaded the stand's owners to let him start a chain of fast-service restaurants with the same name. In 1955 he opened the first McDonald's™ restaurant in the Chicago suburb of Des Plaines, Illinois.

The McDonald's™ Corporation now operates one of the largest fast-food chains, with over 26,000 restaurants in about 120 countries. Its headquarters is located in the Chicago suburb of Oak Brook, Illinois.

**L** can be Lake Michigan.
Its shores let beaches thrive.
To visit, use another "L,"
Chicago's Lake Shore Drive.

Lake Michigan is one of the five Great Lakes of North America, and is the only one located entirely within the United States. The other four are shared with Canada. Lake Michigan has a surface area of 22,400 square miles, making it the largest lake entirely within one country and the fifth largest lake in the world. It is 307 miles long, 118 miles wide, and 923 feet deep, with a shoreline that is 1,640 miles long.

Twelve million people live along Lake Michigan's shores. Chicago's Lake Michigan beaches are known for their beauty and bustling activity. Much of Chicago's 29 miles of city waterfront consists of parks, beaches, residential housing, and historical and cultural attractions.

Lake Shore Drive runs parallel with and alongside the shoreline of Lake Michigan through Chicago. Many famous cultural and civic attractions can be found along Lake Shore Drive. Some of these include The Chicago Yacht Club, Navy Pier, Grant Park, The Museum Campus, and The Museum of Science and Industry.

L1

# M m

The mile-long section of Michigan Avenue north of the Chicago River was dubbed the "Magnificent Mile" in 1947. This area received the nickname because of its many elegant stores, hotels, theaters, restaurants, and office buildings. This shopping and tourist area is popular with Chicagoans and out-of-town guests alike.

The Tribune Tower, the office of the *Chicago Tribune* newspaper, is a distinctive building located on the Magnificent Mile. In 1922 the *Chicago Tribune* hosted an international design competition for its new headquarters and offered a $50,000 prize for "the most beautiful and eye-catching building in the world." Prior to the building of the Tribune Tower, correspondents for the *Chicago Tribune* brought back stones and bricks from a variety of historically important sites throughout the world as they traveled for stories they were reporting on for the newspaper. Many of these have been incorporated into the lowest levels of the building and labeled with their location of origin. In all, there are 136 fragments in the building from such sites as the Alamo, Abraham Lincoln's Tomb, the Parthenon, the Great Pyramids of Egypt, the Great Wall of China, the Berlin Wall, Notre Dame, and the Taj Mahal.

Chicago's famous Magnificent Mile
is a perfect double **M**.
The finest shops define this strip.
Be sure to visit them.

Chicagoans love Navy Pier. This family pavilion, meant strictly for amusement and recreation, claims to be the most-visited attraction in Chicago, with more than 8 million visitors each year.

The 3,000-foot-long pier, set on twenty thousand timber piles, was originally built in 1916 and juts out into Lake Michigan. Navy Pier was originally intended to be a docking and recreational facility, a twin purpose it fulfilled well until the 1930s, when shipping traffic on the Great Lakes dwindled. During World War II it served as a naval training center, and from 1946 to 1965 as the headquarters of the Chicago branch of the University of Illinois, which was later relocated.

During the 1970s and 1980s the pier fell into disuse. The city of Chicago decided in the early 1990s to complete a full-scale renovation, which was finished in 1995. Today the pier includes shops and restaurants, a 150-foot-tall Ferris wheel, a huge tented outdoor theater where popular musical performances take place, a winter skating rink, a botanical garden, the Chicago Children's Museum, and the Chicago Shakespeare Theater.

N
n

Chicago's top attraction for visitors each year? An **N** that's loved by locals, too— of course, it's Navy Pier.

A well-known Midwest gateway
when traveling by air
provides an **O** that pilots know,
Chicago's own—O'Hare.

Originally named Orchard Airport/Douglas Field, the nation's second busiest airport was built between 1942 and 1943 as a manufacturing plant for the Douglas Aircraft Company during World War II. The site was chosen for its proximity to the city of Chicago. In 1945 the airport took the name Orchard Field Airport because of the departure of Douglas, which moved to the west coast.

The airport was renamed in 1949 after Lieutenant Commander Edward "Butch" O'Hare, a World War II flying ace who was awarded the Congressional Medal of Honor in 1942, as well as three other combat citations. O'Hare was a true American hero. According to military historians, O'Hare was a "Top Gun" Navy pilot who shot down five Japanese bombers and crippled a sixth bomber two months after the attack on Pearl Harbor.

Today, O'Hare International Airport is simply known to Chicagoans as O'Hare. The airport welcomes more than 70 million passengers per year and operates an average of 2,500 flights per day. O'Hare has a strong international presence with flights to more than 60 foreign destinations.

# P p

Proudly referred to as Chicago's "front yard," Grant Park is among the city's loveliest and most prominent parks. The park was named for Ulysses S. Grant, 18th president of the United States. The site of three world-class museums—the Art Institute, the Field Museum, and the Shedd Aquarium—the park, which covers about 300 acres, hosts many notable concerts and events. In November of 2008, Barack Obama used the venue to give his historic victory speech following his election as president of the United States.

Grant Park's centerpiece, often referred to as Chicago's "front door" is the Clarence Buckingham Memorial Fountain. The Fountain was built in 1927 to provide a monumental focal point while protecting the park's breath-taking lakefront views. The fountain, one of the largest in the world, is one of Chicago's most popular attractions. While in operation, every hour on the hour for 20 minutes the fountain produces a major water display, and the center jet shoots 150 feet into the air. Beginning at dusk, the water display is accompanied by a major light and music display.

Buckingham Memorial Fountain
majestically lit in the dark
is the centerpiece of a well-known P,
Chicago's beloved Grant Park.

Q is for Quickest—
Duryea's fast car.
He won a big race
though he didn't go far.

Although Henry Ford receives most of the credit for the development of the automobile, America's first gasoline-powered commercial car manufacturers were two brothers, Charles and Frank Duryea. The brothers built their first car in 1893, and it could reach a top speed of 7.5 miles per hour. The following year Frank developed a second car that contained a more powerful two-cylinder engine. It was this car he drove in America's first automobile race held in Chicago, Illinois.

In November 1895, Thanksgiving Day, six motor cars left Chicago's Jackson Park for a 54 mile race to Evanston, Illinois and back through the snow. Car Number 5, driven by inventor Frank Duryea, won the race in just over 10 hours at an average speed of 7.3 miles per hour, and he took home a prize of $2,000.

Charles Duryea founded the Duryea Motor Wagon Company in 1896, the first company to manufacture and sell gasoline-powered vehicles to the public. Like the Wright brothers, the Duryeas were bicycle mechanics with a passion for innovation.

Chicago's R just can't be beat.
It's Reading down on south State Street.
The Harold Washington Library
is such a wondrous place to be.

The Chicago Public Library is one of the nation's largest public library systems. It has millions of books, microfilms, tapes, films, and periodicals. The library system consists of dozens of branches and reading centers. The Great Chicago Fire destroyed the main library downtown in 1871. However, the library was restarted the following year when the British people donated 8,000 books to the city. The main public branch, located south of the loop, is called the Harold Washington Library Center. It is named in honor of Chicago's first African-American mayor.

Many private libraries in Chicago specialize in specific subjects, such as history or science. The Newberry Library is one of the nation's leading historical research libraries. The John Crerar Library at the University of Chicago has wonderful collections in both science and technology. The Art Institute of Chicago houses extensive collections on art and architecture in its Ryerson and Burnham libraries. Lastly, the Chicago History Museum has fine materials regarding Chicago history.

A trio of famous Sculptures provide Chicago an **S**—
The Flamingo, the "Bean," and an unnamed Picasso leave city visitors very impressed.

Visiting Chicago's outdoor sculptures is a popular downtown activity. One of the Loop's most popular sculptures is the famously unnamed Picasso which is located at the Daley Center Plaza. People are compelled to ask an eternal question that is never answered: What does the Picasso represent? Some say the sculpture looks like the face of a woman, while others suggest it could be a baboon.

An interesting steel beam sculpture created by Alexander Calder called The Flamingo is located at the Federal Building Plaza. Its large size and bright red-orange color make it impossible to miss. Its unique shape explains how it received its name.

Cloud Gate, a sculpture by British artist Anish Kapoor, is located in Chicago's Millennium Park. Built between 2004 and 2006, the sculpture is nicknamed "The Bean" because of its legume-like shape. Its highly polished exterior allows it to function like a fun-house mirror. Cloud Gate is 33 feet high, 66 feet long, weighs 110 tons, and cost $23 million to complete.

The Old Water Tower, a Chicago landmark, stands at Michigan and Chicago Avenues. The stone tower, which looks more like a thirteenth century castle than a water tower, was built in 1869. It is the second oldest water tower in the United States. The water tower was the only public building from the Great Chicago Fire burn zone to survive and is the only one of the surviving structures still standing.

The John Hancock Center is a 100-story skyscraper that is recognized around the world for its distinctive architecture, prestigious location, and presence on Chicago's skyline. The 44th-floor sky lobby features America's highest swimming pool. The building itself reaches 1,127 feet in height, and it is 1,506 feet to the top of the antennas.

A skyscraper is an extremely tall building with dozens of floors where thousands of people live or work. The world's first skyscraper was erected in Chicago in 1885. After the Chicago Fire of 1871, with the city in ruins, buildings needed to be replaced. Land prices were high, so taller buildings provided more rooms for offices while using less land.

T for Towers standing tall
creating Chi-town's view.
The Hancock Center's one to note;
The Water Tower, too.

Chicago comes by its reputation as the nation's rail capital quite naturally. At the turn of the last century, Chicago had no fewer than seven major passenger rail terminals and more than 20 separate operational railroads within the city. The most famous of these seven terminals is Chicago's Union Station.

At more than 9 city blocks, the enormous project of building the station took more than 10 years to complete. On May 16, 1925, Union Station opened as a dual structure train station—one part concourse and one part the familiar passenger waiting area and grand hall. The Great Hall welcomes visitors to Chicago with grandeur and purpose.

Chicago's Union Station is a busy place with upward of 100,000 passengers on the city's Metra commuter rail and Amtrak passing through its halls daily. Today, Union Station is home to many of Amtrak's most famous trains, including the California Zephyr.

U u

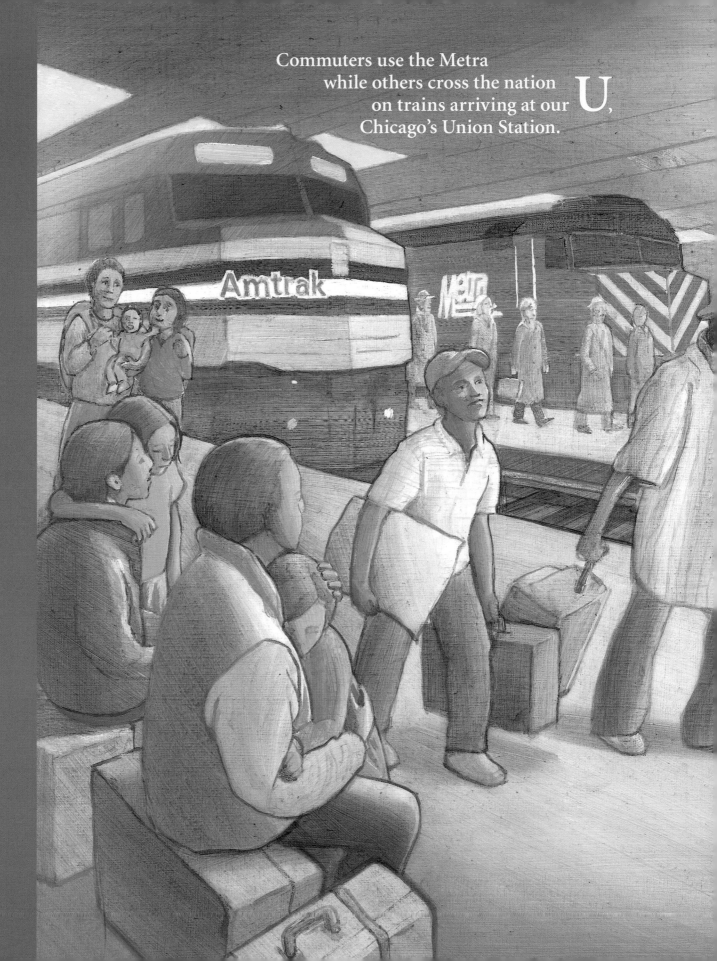

Commuters use the Metra while others cross the nation on trains arriving at our **U**, Chicago's Union Station.

Chicago's population is made up of immigrants and different ethnic groups. By the 1970s, immigrant groups had come from countries such as Poland, Italy, Germany, and Sweden. Today, the largest ethnic group is African-American, with the Hispanic community growing quickly. Many immigrant groups established communities based on their culture. Little Italy, Greek Town, and Chinatown are a few immigrant neighborhoods. Bridgeport and Pilsen are home to Latin Americans. Old Town was settled by Germans.

Chicago's diverse ethnic population offers a wide variety of delicious foods. Chicago is famous for its deep dish pizza, Chicago style hot dogs, Wrigley's Gum, and Eli's cheesecake. Every summer the "Taste of Chicago" festival draws millions of people who want to sample many types of ethnic cuisine.

African-American musicians brought a soulful style of music called "The Blues" to Chicago. Blues music expresses both sadness and hope. Chicago's annual Blues Festival held in Grant Park celebrates old favorites and welcomes new talent.

The DuSable Museum of African American History is one of several Chicago museums that celebrates the city's diverse ethnic and cultural heritage. The museum is named for Jean Baptiste Point DuSable. In 1779 DuSable established a trading post and settlement that would later become known as Chicago.

V is for Variety
in culture and ethnicity.
Diversity—Chicago's got—
the city is a melting pot.

Why do people call one of the most magnificent cities in the Midwest "The Windy City?" Many assume the nickname refers to the blustery or "windy" weather experienced in Chicago. People have debated other possible origins and meanings. One theory claims the nickname comes from New York newspaper editor Charles Dana. According to the theory, Mr. Dana coined the phrase in 1893 when he claimed that Chicago politicians were full of "wind" because they bragged so much about their city's outstanding attributes while bidding to become hosts for the 1893 World's Fair. The nickname stuck. No matter which explanation one believes, the truth is that people all over the world refer to Chicago as "The Windy City."

Chicago's **W** is for
a nickname we can't hide.
The famous Windy City
is known both far and wide.

X marks this spot, and
Chicago pride will fill us.
The problem? It's our tower's name,
is it Sears...or Willis?

In 1974 the Sears Tower became the world's tallest skyscraper at 1,454 feet high. It consists of 9 connected towers and stands 110 stories tall. The building contains more than 100 elevators and has 4.5 million square feet of space. The tower is so large it has its own zip code. In 2005 the *Chicago Tribune* reported that readers had named the Sears Tower one of the "Seven Wonders of Chicago."

For 22 years the Sears Tower held the record for the world's tallest building. While it is still the tallest building in the United States, it is no longer the tallest building in the world. The honor now goes to Malaysia's Petronas Twin Towers at 1,483 feet tall.

In March of 2009 London-based Willis Group Holdings, Ltd. struck a deal with the firm that owns the Sears Tower for exclusive naming rights to the building. The imposing skyscraper was officially renamed "Willis Tower" on July 16, 2009. While the name on the building may indeed say Willis Tower, in the hearts of many Chicagoans it will forever remain the Sears Tower.

The Chicago Yacht Club is proud to have a long-standing tradition of yachting excellence. *Yachting Magazine* declared it "one of the country's most distinguished yacht clubs." The club's goal is to advance the community's knowledge, enjoyment, and participation in boating.

The Chicago Yacht Club is the most famous organizer and host of regattas, races, and other contests in the United States. No other yacht club presents more national-level races. The yacht club's most famous event is the Race to Mackinac, which is the longest annual freshwater sailing race in the world, and the year 2008 marked the 100th running of this prestigious race.

The annual 333-mile Race to Mackinac begins off the mouth of the Chicago River just east of Navy Pier in Chicago, crosses Lake Michigan, barely enters Lake Huron, and finishes in the Round Island Channel, off Mackinac Island, Michigan. Hundreds of sailboats enter the race each year.

Founded in 1875
Chicago Yacht Club is our Y.
Its members all want to promote
good times and safety on a boat.

Yy

Brookfield Zoo covers approximately 216 acres and houses around 450 species (3,100 specimens) of animals in natural settings. The zoo officially opened on June 30, 1934, and quickly gained international recognition. The zoo was the first in America to exhibit giant pandas. Brookfield Zoo also built the nation's first fully-indoor dolphin exhibit, and in the 1980s the zoo introduced Tropic World, the first fully-indoor rain forest simulation and the then-largest indoor zoo exhibit. The zoo is managed by the Chicago Zoological Society, which sponsors numerous research and conservation efforts globally.

Lincoln Park Zoo, located in Lincoln Park—one of Chicago's largest and most well-known parks, was established in 1868 with the gift of a pair of swans from New York's Central Park. The park is also described as "a world of wildlife in the shadow of skyscrapers." A leader in research and education, the zoo is open 365 days a year and offers free admission to all.

Zz

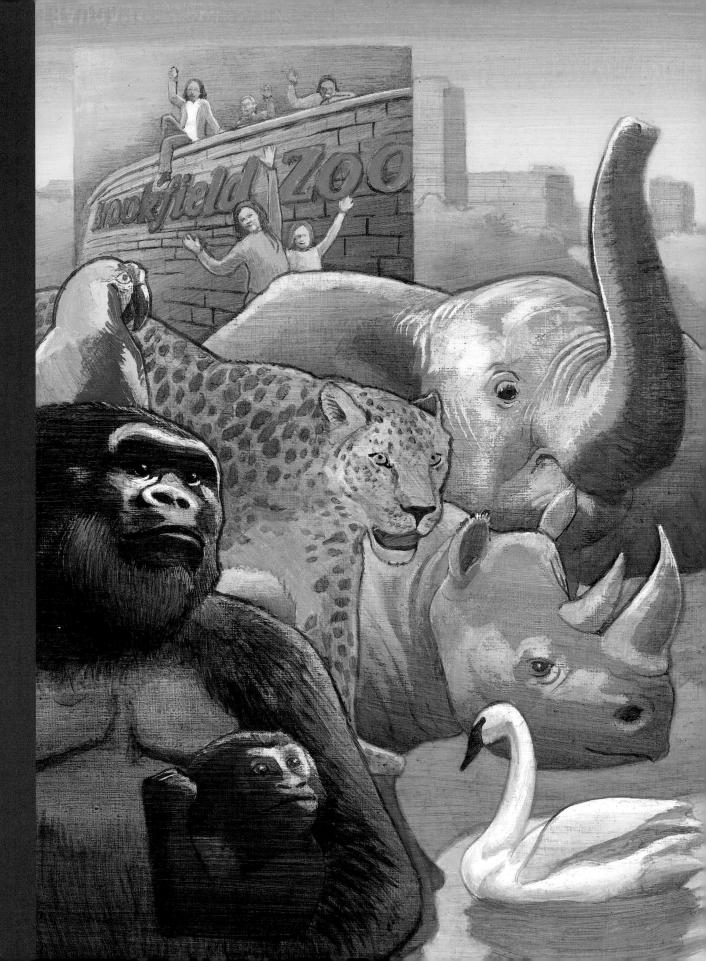

Any major city's **Z**
would likely be its Zoo.
Chicago sets the bar quite high
it has not one—but two.

Lincoln Park
Zoo

# Bibliography

Bjarkman, P. C. (1994). *Ernie Banks*. New York: Chelsea House Publishers.

Bloomberg, K. (1999). Illinois State Library Special Report: Illinois African-American Resource Guide, Vol. 6, No. 2. Springfield, IL: Illinois State Library.

Blushfield, J. F. (2003). *Oprah Winfrey*. Milwaukee: World Almanac Library.

Borger, S. (2007). Chicago's Union Station: A Monument to Rail Travel. Rail Magazine, 18, 30-33. Retrieved April 18, 2009 from http://www.ctaa.org/ct/archives.asp.

Brill, M. T. (2006). *Barack Obama: Working to Make a Difference*. Minneapolis, MN: Millbrook Press.

Cooper, F. (2004). *Jump: From the Life of Michael Jordan*. New York: Philome Books.

Davis, L. (1993). Kidding Around Chicago: A Young Person's Guide. New York: W.W. Norton and Company, Inc.

Doherty, C. A., & Doherty, M. (1995). *The Sears Tower*. Woodbridge, CT: Blackbirch Press, Inc.

Feinstein, S. (2008). *African-American Heroes: Barack Obama*. Berkeley Heights, NJ: Enslow Publishers, Inc.

Feinstein, S. (2008). *African-American Heroes: Oprah Winfrey*. Berkeley Heights, NJ: Enslow Publishers, Inc.

Furstinger, N. (2005). *Chicago*. Edina, MN: ABDO Publishing Company.

Glusac, E., Kronish, E., & Sotonoff, R. (2008). *DK Eyewitness Top 10 Travel Guides: Chicago*. New York: DK Publishing, Inc.

Grossman, J. R., Keating, A. D., & Reiff, J. L. (2004). *The Encyclopedia of Chicago*. Chicago: The University of Chicago Press.

Honig, D. (1991). *The Chicago Cubs: An Illustrated History*. New York: Prentice Hall Press.

Hurd, O. (2007). *Chicago History for Kids: Triumphs and Tragedies of the Windy City*. Chicago: Chicago Review Press, Inc.

Kroc, R. A. (1977). *Grinding It Out: The Making of McDonald's*. Chicago: Henry Regnery Company.

Krohn, K. (2005). *Oprah Winfrey*. Minneapolis: Lerner Publications Company.

Landau, E. (2001). *Skyscrapers*. New York: Children's Press.

Littman, M. (2008). *The Little Black Book of Chicago*. White Plains, NY: Peter Pauper Press, Inc.

Love, J. F. (1986). *McDonald's: Behind the Arches*. New York: Bantam Books.

Maes, N. (2002). *Around Chicago with Kids*. New York: Fodor's Travel Publications.

Marx, C. (2004). *The Great Chicago Fire of 1871*. New York: The Rosen Publishing Group, Inc.

McCormick, L. W. (2007). *Michael Jordan*. New York: Children's Press.

McShane, C. (1997). *The Automobile*. Westport, CT: Greenwood Press.

Nagle, J. (2008). *Oprah Winfrey: Profile of a Media Mogul*. New York: The Rosen Publishing Group, Inc.

Nobleman, M. T. (2005). *Great Cities of the World: Chicago*. Milwaukee: World Almanac Library.

Ochterbeck, C. C. (2006). *Chicago Must-Sees*. Greenville, SC: Michelin Travel Publications.

Oxlade, C. (2001). *Building Amazing Structures: Skyscrapers*. Chicago: Heinemann Library.

Phelps, K. (1992). *The Young People's Atlas of the United States*. New York: Kingfisher Books.

Phillips, S. I. (2005). *Museums of Chicago*. Yardley, PA: Westholme Publishing, LLC.

Schulze, F., & Harrington, K. (2003). *Famous Chicago Buildings*. Chicago: The University of Chicago Press.

Shuman, M. A. (2008). *Barack Obama: We Are One People*. Berkeley Heights, NJ: Enslow Publishers, Inc.

Sinkevitch, A. (2004). *AIA Guide to Chicago*. New York: Harcourt, Inc.

Stein, R. C. (1997). *Cities of the World: Chicago*. New York: Children's Press.

Stein, R. C. (2005). *The Great Chicago Fire*. New York: Children's Press.

Visalli, S. (2003). *Chicago*. New York: Universe Publishing.

*The World Book Encyclopedia*. (2008). Chicago: Worldbook, Inc.

Zschock, M. D. (2005). *Journey around Chicago from A to Z*. Beverly, MA: Commonwealth Editions.

http://www.chicagoyachtclub.org